Published by Stratford Living Publishing.

ISBN Print: 978-1-990332-52-4

Dedicated to Avery

Mommy and Daddy tell us it's important

To try new foods - like stew

I don't mind
most of the time

Except when there's an ewww in my stew!

I could close my eyes and try it

I could pretend it's something yummy

But I'd have to plug my

to fool my tummy!

Instead I think I'll just JUMP JUMP JUMP and SAY EWWW TO STEW!

But something is happening in my bowl....

It's bubbling and twisting in front of me!

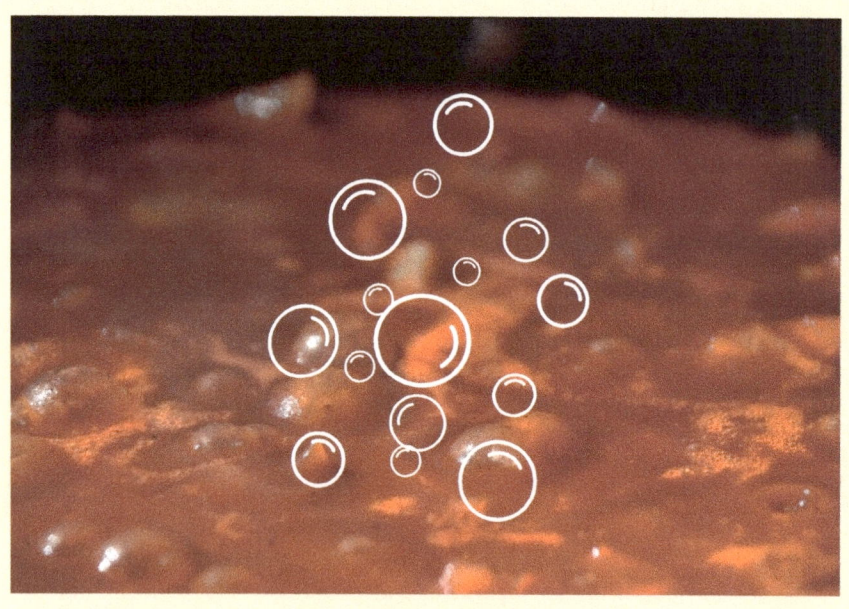

Wait a minute -
letters appear -
I count them 1, 2, 3.

Then more letters...

Churning and turning

Moving and grooving

An

is in my ewww stew.

Then a

And another

An

And an

My ewww stew spells APPLE

I like APPLES!

I take a spoonful - but
no matter what I do -
It's still ewww stew!

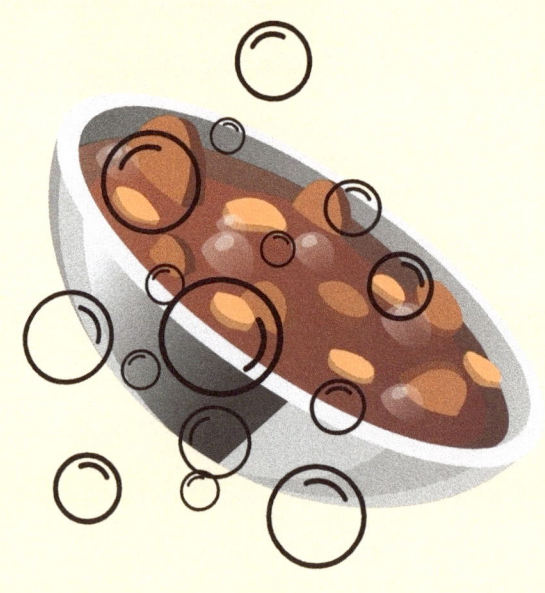

Soon the letters churn and spit

The hot ewww stew hits my eye and I yell

"What's the matter?" Daddy asks.

I rub my eye not knowing what to say

Soon more letters appear

Mommy asks, "Is it too hot?"

I shake my head as the letters twist into ANT

I JUMP JUMP JUMP BECAUSE

THERE IS AN ANT in my EWWW STEW!

The ant word clears

New letters appear

GREEN GOO

is in my EWWW STEW!

Under the table my brother kicks me in the shin

As the letters twist and turn again into:

I JUMP JUMP JUMP BECAUSE NOW THERE IS

ORANGE GOOP IN MY EWWW STEW!

I cover my face.

"If you don't like Stew," Mommy says

"It's perfectly okay. You can give it a try on another day."

A winking face appears in the EWWW STEW

I JUMP JUMP JUMP and WAVE GOODBYE TO EWWW STEW!

I
DIDN'T

EWWW
STEW
TODAY!

Jump Series:
Jump Like a Caribou!
Jump Like a Kangaroo!
Jump at the Zoo!
Jump and Say P.U.!
Jump and Say Boo!
Jump and Say Valentine's Day Is
For Kids Too!
Jump and Look For a Clue
Jump and Say Happy Birthday to You!
Jump For Everything Blue!
Jump and Say Cock-A-Doodle-Do!
Jump and Squawk Like a Cockatoo
Jump and Ask Is It Ewe?
Jump and Say Merry Christmas to You!
Other Children's Books:
The Three Boulders
Billy Shakespeare
Billie Shakespeare

.